Discovering Your Ministry Identity

by Paul R. Ford

Learning To Be Who You Already Are !

For Teams, Groups, or Individuals

Published by ChurchSmart Resources

We are an evangelical Christian publisher committed to producing excellent products at affordable prices to help church leaders accomplish effective ministry in the areas of Church planting, Church growth, Church renewal and Leadership development.

For a free catalog of our resources call **1-800-253-4276**.

Discovering Your Ministry Identity
For Teams, Groups, or Individuals
by Paul R. Ford

Printed in the United States of America

ISBN 1-889638-07-2

Paul Ford continues to create helpful tools for mobilizing people in ministry. Discovering Your Ministry Identity is no exception, building on previous writings and adding new material that provides a good resource for personal and team development.

I remember meeting Paul a number of years ago when my wife and I were developing systems for spiritual gifts mobilization. Paul's passion to help people find the right ministry roles came through strongly in our interactions. I have appreciated the way which he continues to develop practical tools that make significant contributions to further the application of gift theology in local churches and other ministries. His written works reflect insights that flow out of the crucible of ministry experience.

I particularly like the way Paul has woven several areas together in this new resource, including discipleship, spiritual gifts, leadership style and personal values. Discovering Your Ministry Identity is full of practical exercises that will help you to take a multi-faceted approach that helps people think about themselves and their team members more holistically.

Discovering Your Ministry Identity is a wonderful toolkit for team building. As you work through the exercises, you will increase your understanding of yourself and others on your team. Not only will you find out how you may be effective on a team, but you may also discover quite accurately who you need to make you more effective. The surveys and discussion questions are designed for maximum flexibility. As you communicate with your team members, you will have one or more "ah-ha" experiences.

You will find this workbook to be valuable for your ministry. I recommend that you use it personally and with your team to cultivate greater ministry effectiveness.

For the advancement of God's kingdom together,

Bob Logan
Executive Director, CoachNet
September 1998

I dedicate this book to my wife,
Julie Margaret LeClear Ford,
with whom I have re-discovered
the grace and love of God
over the past three years.

TABLE OF CONTENTS

3

TABLE OF CONTENTS

Introduction **5**

The Individual Discovery Process **6**

Apostle Paul's Ministry Identity Revealed **6**

My Search **7**

The Team Discovery Process **8**

The Discovery Tools: **9**
Assessment Exercises included in this workbook

- **The Discipleship Triangle:** **10**
  How is your spiritual fitness today?

- **Heights Spiritual Gifts Survey:** **12**
  Do you have Equipping, supporting and/or prayer/worship gifts?

- **Here's What I Think of You!** **24**
  Get personal feedback on your spiritual gifts.

- **Team Style Questionnaire:** **26**
  How do you function on a team?

- **What is Your Ministry Burden or Passion?** **30**
  In who, in what or where do you want to invest your life?

- **Your Vital Values:** **31**
  What is most and least important to you?

- **Principle Priorities of Leadership:** *(Optional)* **37**
  What are you good at and who do you need?
  Especially helpful for leadership teams.

- **Teamshredding Attitudes:** *(Optional)* **38**
  What are your shredding techniques?

Summary: Focusing Your Ministry Identity **39**
Summarize all the pieces in two pages

Appendix A **41**
Spiritual Gift Definitions & Characteristics

4

For by grace you have been saved, through faith –
and this is not from yourselves, it is the gift of God –
not by works, so that no one can boast. For we are God's
workmanship, created in Christ Jesus to do good works,
which God prepared in advance for us to do.
Ephesians 2:8-10

As you search for significance in your life, remember: it is not what you do for God that is important. Rather, it is learning to be who you already are in Christ! Discovering who you are in Christ is one of the most important journeys you will make in your Christian life. Since there is no one else in the Body of Christ quite like you, discovering your ministry identity – who you already are in Christ – is absolutely essential.

If you look closely at Ephesians 2:10, you will read that we do not DO the workmanship of God, but rather we ARE the workmanship of God, created in Christ Jesus for good works. Each of us has been prepared by God to be who He wants us to be. What steps can you take to intentionally discover your ministry identity, the workmanship of God already in place in your life? Whether you are a rookie or veteran Christian, come along on your own further discovery of God's internal crafting!

Picture a beautifully hand-crafted book case, a true work of art accomplished by a well known craftsmen in your area. What does a book case say? "Look at me! See how well I hold these books in place!" Well, not exactly. A bookcase does not say that. A book case simply stands there, reflecting the incredible craftsmanship of its creator.

As Christians, that is exactly what you and I do! Through your Ministry Identity, the workmanship is already in place in you just as God determined. You are ready to reflect the incredible craftsmanship of your Creator. It is a process of discovering and fulfilling the design components which the Lord has strategically placed in you. It is not learning new things you ought to do as a Christian. It is, rather, learning to fulfill who and what God has already prepared.[1]

Consider Fred, the craftsman. He was a carpenter who trained apprentices. But he also had the gift of pastoring. As Fred began to discover his ministry identity, he ended up encouraging hundreds of others as he became the foreman for building 25 Habitat for Humanity houses. I wish you could have watched Fred pastor others on those roofs and in those hallways. He was that book case, reflecting the craftsmanship of his Creator. He learned to be himself, a true work of art, in the Kingdom of God.

Discover your Ministry Identity. You will have the opportunity to go step-by-step through each strategic part of your ministry identity in the following pages. If you are considering how you fit with others on a ministry team or in a small group, you will have the body building chance to discover who you are and how you function in fulfilling God's purposes through your team, group, or church.

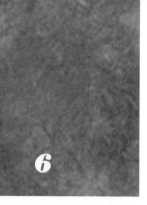

6

I have worked with Christians from Los Angeles to Moscow to Bombay, with hundreds of stops in between. I can tell you with great confidence that Christians everywhere are searching to find their significance in Christ. The search is particularly dramatic in the West. North America, with its material trappings, exercise fanaticism, and dream vacations, has become a center in this search for meaning. Frantic busyness has replaced a sense of community for many as they search for their next exciting life event. Also, many are trying to work their way toward a sense of deeper meaning and personal fulfillment.

But what if you and I really are the workmanship of God, created in Christ Jesus for good works, as Ephesians 2:10 states? What if our significance has already been settled at the cross of Jesus Christ, where He died for the sins of each of us? Take note of Ephesians 2:8-9, the important lead-in to 2:10. You and I are saved by grace, and, as the passage says, not by you (verse 8) or your works (verse 9). It is God's free gift of grace undeservedly offered to each of us who are unable to earn it on our own. Yet He freely offers it. We do not, cannot, work for it.

What if the process is actually one of discovering that which already exists in each of us? Ephesians 2:10 reveals the beginning step of our search. As we respond to His grace, each of us becomes the very workmanship of God. He "graces" us with His favor, and we are already prepared by the Father to be His workmanship. We do not have to go to school to learn how to serve Him. Our service grows out of who we already are. His grace has already fitted us with tools of the Kingdom of God.

How can we describe God's workmanship in us? I call it Ministry Identity: not what you do for God, but who you already are in Christ. The potential God has built into each of us is so much more amazing and wonderful than any Christian service we could ever perform on our own. It has become a part of the fabric of your being! Each of us has a portion of God's grace already empowered and ready to function as an extension of who we are.

What are the key elements of this Ministry Identity?

THE APOSTLE PAUL'S MINISTRY IDENTITY REVEALED

We find an excellent starting point in the life and ministry of the Apostle Paul through Romans 15:15-20. As Paul talks about his Christian service, parts of his ministry identity are clearly shown. The first vital piece is his spiritual giftedness. In fact, the root word of "spiritual gift" in the New Testament is "grace."[2] In other words, when we are saved by God's grace, each one of us is literally "graced" with specific abilities called spiritual gifts. That is why you will find the word grace in every passage on spiritual gifts in the New Testament. God truly endowed each of us with a part of His grace.

Paul exposes at least two of his spiritual gifts as he shares about his service: evangelism and the apostolic gift.[3] The first is revealed as he talks about proclaiming the Gospel in such a way that people respond. He mentions this at least four times in the passage. His foundation-building comment in verse 20 clearly hints at the apostolic gift, as does the signs and wonders reference in verse 18.[4] In other words, as Paul shares about his service to God, his spiritually gifted areas move to the forefront of the activities most on his heart. Paul's gifts are not only obvious in his words, but also obvious in the fruit born in the functioning of those gifts as revealed in the New Testament book of Acts. More than just good training or a developed set of skills, it was the power of God at work. It was an extension of Paul's ministry identity.

The second vital component of Paul's Ministry Identity was his ministry burden or passion. The passage shows Paul obviously had a tremendous heart for the Gentiles, or "non-Jews." It was a deep burden that just would not go away. It was his passion in that he was willing to invest his very life in the Gentiles time and again as modeled in the book of Acts. It was not as if he did not care for

the Jews. Rather he was compelled to seek out Gentiles so they could respond to Jesus Christ!

There are other significant pieces that are part of your Ministry Identity makeup. We will cover those shortly. You will have opportunity to assess yourself and even other members of your group or team, should this be a shared process for you.

What is important is to clearly understand that, as with the Apostle Paul, God has already made you to be his workmanship in specific, identifiable ways. You and I are just like Paul, only different. Each of us is unique because the part we play in the Body of Christ is different according to God's design. We can indeed discover and fulfill the workmanship that is a part of who we are.

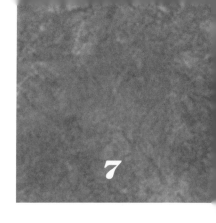

MY SEARCH

I am a preacher's kid of a preacher's kid, and the last thing in the world I wanted to do vocationally was to become a full time minister. But I experienced a distinct sense of calling which, in those days, meant going to Christian seminary or Bible school to be trained as a pastor. I spent four years preparing to be a minister and then moved into a pastoral position. After 10 years and two pastoral roles, it became clear to me that I was not a good fit for the traditional role of minister. But what to do? I believed I was called as a Christian and did indeed have spiritual gifts, but what could I DO?

I began to realize I enjoyed equipping others and then releasing them into meaningful service (Ephesians 4:11-12.) I loved to assist them in discovering their place! I found great joy in calling people to discover their significance in the Body of Christ, to understand that each is a player, even if they have no special training. I also realized that I loved to invest my life in college singles in their twenties. I also found tremendous joy investing in and encouraging other Christian leaders, many of whom were searching to find their own significance.

In fact, having worked with over 5,000 Christian leaders, I know that many, of them are struggling to find their place of significance in the Body of Christ. I can help such leaders discover and fulfill their ministry identity rather than trying to fill some impossible ministry role or perform service in hopes of becoming significant. It is not what I do for God, but rather learning to be who I already am in Christ.

Then I found Romans 15:15-20 and discovered I had a unique Ministry Identity just like every other Christian. I determined, through study and confirmation from other Christians, that I was a gifted exhorter-leader who had a deep burden to invest my life in college singles in their twenties and leaders in transition. I now understood why I so enjoyed, and still enjoy, the activities mentioned in the last two paragraphs. Those are a part of my workmanship, God's intricate crafting of me to be just who He wanted me to be. I am uniquely prepared to play my part in God's Kingdom plan to win the world, and now I am on a crusade to help others learn to do the same.

How about you? What are your spiritual gifts? There are many things you do well, but only two or three you do supernaturally on a consistent basis. That is why spiritual giftedness is the first and driving component of the Ministry Identity puzzle. In whom or what or where do you want to invest your life–your ministry burden or passion? What other distinctions are a part of your Ministry Identity? That is the process before you.

Some surprises lie ahead. Remember the move from "what I do is important" to "who I am is essential" is most significant if you are going to find your Ministry Identity. Reread Ephesians 2:8-10 if you need a healthy reminder. Some veteran Christians going through this ministry identity assessment process will discover their gifts and burdens may be somewhat different or a lot different than what they believed up until now. Most of us have been asked to fill ministry slots for most of our faith walk, and we never stopped to seriously evaluate those unique and supernatural puzzle pieces which make up the real you and me.

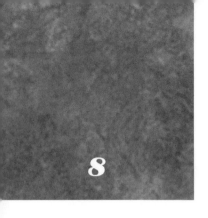

In one of my favorite movies, "Dead Poets Society," a young school teacher – portrayed by Robin Williams – seeks to motivate his students about literature in dramatic and creative ways. At one point, Williams begins to whisper these words in an attempt to captivate his students, "Carpe Diem." "Seize the day!"

Today is your opportunity to discover and fulfill your ministry identity! Today is the day to consider intently who you are in Christ after years of serving in the church, perhaps with little joy or fruit experienced in your service. Or you never have understood why you experienced joy in doing a certain activity. Today is a new chance to gain insight about yourself as you share with others your Ministry Identity assessment results for their honest feedback. Today may be the day when you begin to learn "no" is a spiritual word; that is, you may need to consider moving out of present ministry responsibilities and move into an area that has long been on your heart.

"Seize the day!"

THE TEAM DISCOVERY PROCESS

While you will discover many personal insights working through the "Ministry Identity Assessment Process" on your own, the greatest potential benefit may come by going through this discovery process with others. In fact, the best way to confirm your Ministry Identity is in the context of meaningful relationships. Whether it be a ministry team or cell group or close knit accountability group, working through this process with others who know you well is a definite advantage!

Why? Consider the following verses from key New Testament passages in Romans and 1 Corinthians:

"Just as each of us has one body with many members, and these members do not all have the same function, so in Christ we who are many form one body, and each member belongs to all the others."[5]

"But in fact, God has arranged the parts in the body, every one of them, just as He wanted them to be. If they were all one part, where would the body be? As it is, there are many parts, but one body."[6]

Being a Christian automatically includes belonging to the Body of Christ. You and I have become an integral part of and play distinct parts in the Body of Christ, just as God determined. If this is true, as the Apostle Paul tells us, then discovering each of our places is more than just one person finding his or her individual place. I find my place in the Body of Christ in relationship to others in the Body, and vice versa. I would go so far as to say God's primary setting for revealing ministry identity is in the midst of relationships with other Christians.[7]

So then, are there other Christians in your life who would benefit by going through this assessment and discovery process with you? Are you a part of a ministry team, cell group, task force or accountability group with whom you could interact about insights you gain concerning your ministry identity? All involved would benefit from the insights of others, but more importantly, each could gain a greater sense of how your individual ministry identities may fit in the larger Body of Christ.

Imagine many different parts of the Body of Christ individually understanding how each fits with other parts to make up an arm or a leg as part of the larger Body. What an exciting possibility in the midst of a ruggedly independent culture! Since who I am affects who we are, just as God determines, it makes sense to consider who I am in process with others alongside.

As you look toward discovering or reconfirming your own ministry identity, consider I Peter 4:10: *"Each one should use whatever gift he [she] has received to serve others, faithfully administering God's grace in its various forms."* It is in the context of using your gifts to serve others that God's grace is dispensed. Personal discovery is for the purpose of serving others, not simply for personal understanding. Understanding who I am helps me see my ministry identity fit with others, so that who we are can more clearly fulfill God's purposes in the world.

Discovering Your Ministry Identity

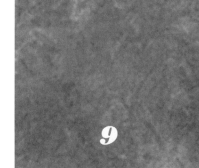

How to Use the "Ministry Identity Assessment Process"

The remainder of this workbook is a series of discovery exercises that give you the opportunity to reflect on your ministry identity. These exercises also provide information for interaction with others who can assist you in making a sober estimate of who you are in Christ.[8] Here is a brief overview of the "Ministry Identity Assessment Tools."

Your Spiritual Fitness Checkup Using The Discipleship Triangle (p. 10): The process of discovering and fulfilling who you are in Christ really starts with your spiritual fitness...your growth in Christ. The "Discipleship Triangle" gives you a chance to look at five important areas in your spiritual growth and how you are doing in each area. In those areas where you are struggling, it also allows you to accountably look at ways to get back on track.

The Heights Spiritual Gifts Survey (p. 12): This gifts inventory helps you determine how you may be gifted, the only part of your personal makeup that acts supernaturally on a consistent basis. Your gifts not only define the ministry roles in which you could serve, but also reveal HOW you will serve or teach or lead. It takes into account experience (what you have done) and motivations (what you would like to try). A person's top two or three gifts are commonly revealed among the top six scores, meaning that comparing results from the other assessment tools is very important in discerning probable gifts.

The Team Style Questionnaire (p. 26): This tool helps people see how they work with others on a team or in a group. Most of us have one or two primary styles we use when working with others, and this assessment helps clarify those styles. It also helps people understand the strengths and liabilities that each brings to the team.

If You Could Create Your Own Ministry (p. 30): This tool is designed to expand your horizons. If you had free opportunity to create something new, what would it be? If spiritual gifts are the supernatural how, this might be the place or people with whom you use those gifts. Some call this ministry identity category your "ministry burden or passion." For example:

- Specific activity?...teaching, feeding the poor, hospital visits or encouraging others.
- Specific group of people?...blue collar workers, single moms, elderly or Asians.
- Specific location?...your home town or neighborhood, Boston (city) or Russia (country).

Your Vital Values (p. 31): What is really important to you? What do you value? Questions answered in this tool evaluate four major areas: values in your work, life and relationships; values important to you as you equip or train others; decision-making values; and team values. Values are essential for you to understand as you approach any area of service or a team ministry opportunity.

Principle Priorities of an Equipper (p. 37): *(Optional)* For those with one or more equipping gifts, this tool is extremely helpful in identifying strengths in five areas that are important for leading, equipping, or training others. This tool identifies what a person does well, and also what skills in others he or she needs to be most effective. Often we think of things which we do well. We seldom think about who we need to make each of us better!

Teamshredders (p. 38): *(Optional)* Another tool related to teamwork, this simple assessment gives you the chance to acknowledge potential weaknesses when working on a team. Because of the extreme honesty required, this resource is most helpful in a team-building process where a high level of honesty has already been established among the group or team.

Endnotes

1. 1 Corinthians 12:18.
2. A Greek word study done on Ephesians 2:8-10 and Romans 12:3-6 reveals the relationship between the words for grace and spiritual gifts.
3. In 2 Timothy 1:11 and 1 Timothy 2:7, the Apostle Paul reveals his God-empowered role, which could appropriately be understood as his spiritual gifts.
4. In 2 Corinthians 12:12, Paul says involvement with signs, wonders and miracles confirms one to be a first century apostle.
5. Romans 5:4-5.
6. 1 Corinthians 12:18-20.
7. For a more in-depth look at discovering one's ministry identity in the context of relationships, see one of my other books, *Unleash Your Church!*, chapter 7, pages 59-64.
8. Romans 12:6. The idea of "making a sober estimate" is discussed more completely in *Unleash Your Church!*, chapter 6, pages 53-58.

Your Spiritual Fitness Checkup Using The Discipleship Triangle

STEP 1: RATE YOUR SPIRITUAL FITNESS

One a scale of 1 (lowest) to 5 (highest), estimate how you are doing in these five essential areas of growth in your Christian life. A disciple is one who follows Jesus, and each of us move from strength to weakness in one area at various times in the seasons of discipleship. Assess how you are doing at present – not how you were doing last week or hope to be doing tomorrow. These five categories are taken from the Discipleship Triangle on the next page.

_____ The center of the Christian life . . . . Abiding in Christ.
Devotional Bible reading.   *Daily prayer.*   *Personal and corporate worship.*

_____ Your deeper time in the Bible . . . . Growing deeper in God's Word.
Bible Study.   *Digging deeper for understanding.*   *Acting on what you read.*

_____ Your significant relationships with other Christians . . . . Accountable relationships.
Encouragement.   *Regular accountability.*   *Committed prayer for each other.*

_____ Your supernatural ministry . . . . Discovering and using your spiritual gifts.
What combination of gifts do you have?   *Exercising your gifts in tandem with others.*

_____ The crucial big picture . . . . Fulfilling the Great Commission.
This part affects each of the other four.   *Make disciples by investing your life in them.*

STEP#2 CHECK OUT IMBALANCE AREAS

Are you putting too much focus on one particular area of your spiritual fitness? Read through the three major areas where too much emphasis is commonly given. If you identify one or two areas where you are out of balance or spending too much time (i.e. making another area weak), place a check mark in that area.

_____ Overfocus on growing deeper in God's Word . . . . Spiritual fatness!
Like overeating, can become sluggish.   *Having all the right answers.*   *Judgmental.*

_____ Overfocus on accountable relationships . . . . Koinonitis!
Too much focus inward on a good group thing!   *Ingrown.*   *No new people reached out to.*

_____ Overfocus on using your spiritual gifts . . . . Burnout!
All focus on serving without abiding in Christ regularly.   *Not accountable - too busy serving!*

ACCOUNTABILITY . . .

Consider these practical action steps with someone:

1. Pray specifically for each other in your areas of strength and weakness.
2. Determine action steps to take in your weakest area and hold each other accountable to those plans.
3. Meet once or twice more to pray for one another and to hold each other accountable.
4. Establish an ongoing group whose purpose is to weekly encourage each member in one or two areas of **The Discipleship Triangle**.

The Discipleship Triangle

Growing Deeper in God's Word
2 Peter 1:3-4; 2 Timothy 3:16-17
• Bible Study
• Doctrine: What and Why You Believe
• Action: Obedience

"The Great Commission" Matthew 28:18-20

"The Great Commission" Matthew 28:18-20

Abiding in Christ
John 15:5-11
• Prayer
• Worship
• Devotional Bible Reading

Accountable Relationships
Acts 2:42-47;
Hebrews 10:24-25
• Accountability
• Vulnerability
• Prayer

"The Great Commission"
Matthew 28:18-20
It Affects Every Part of the Discipleship
Triangle as Our Ultimate Purpose:
Disciple-Making

Discovering/Using Spiritual Gifts
1 Peter 4:10-11;
Ephesians 4:11-16
• Ministry
• Service
• Bodybuilding

Remember: Your spiritual fitness is central to your ministry effectiveness.
Discerning God's will and direction is a day to day, hour to hour proposition.
All the assessment results found on the next pages are tied directly to your
relationship with Jesus Christ. If you need more help in your Christian
walk or want training resources on "Spiritual Fitness Training" based on
The Discipleship Triangle, contact Paul Ford for more information.

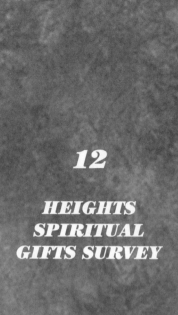

12

HEIGHTS SPIRITUAL GIFTS SURVEY

Heights Spiritual Gifts Survey

The Heights Spiritual Gifts Survey is an exercise to help you discover what your spiritual gifts may be. The concept of a survey was originally published by Richard F. Houts (Eternity, May 1976, paged 18-21) and later modified by C. Peter Wagner of Fuller Evangelistic Association. Paul R. Ford led a team who developed the Heights Spiritual Gifts Survey for use at Heights Cumberland Presbyterian Church in Albuquerque, New Mexico.

First Edition	May 1988
Revised	November 1989
Revised	April 1991
Revised	May 1998

INSTRUCTIONS

Step 1

Read and answer each of the 125 statements by marking the box that corresponds, to the extent the statement is true in your life:

Frequently - 3   **Sometimes - 2**   **Seldom - 1**   **Never - 0**

CAUTION! Do not answer according to what you think should be true or hope might be true in the future. Be honest and answer bases on your experience.

Step 2

When you are finished, score the survey by using the Heights Spiritual Gifts Survey Summary Chart on page 23.

    Discovering Your Ministry Identity

For each statement, mark the box for the description that best applies to your life:

Frequently - 3	Sometimes - 2	Seldom - 1	Never - 0
3	2	1	0

1. I have unusual sensitivity for recognizing thoughts or impressions that are from the Holy Spirit. ☐ ☐ ☐ ☐

2. When the opportunity arises, I seek friendships with those who are culturally and ethnically different from me. ☐ ☐ ☐ ☐

3. I would love the opportunity to go to another country and equip Christians to serve. ☐ ☐ ☐ ☐

4. I respond freely and willingly to requests for financial support of worthy Christian endeavors. ☐ ☐ ☐ ☐

5. I find joy in assuming routine aspects of another's responsibilities to free them for other things. ☐ ☐ ☐ ☐

6. Using knowledge that could not have originated in myself, I recognize situations in which the Spirit wants to work. ☐ ☐ ☐ ☐

7. I see practical tasks that need to be done and do them quietly, without others noticing. ☐ ☐ ☐ ☐

8. I have a great desire to offer encouragement and direction to those who are troubled, distressed, or making important life decisions. ☐ ☐ ☐ ☐

9. When I speak out or provide leadership, people usually listen, agree, and follow my input or guidance. ☐ ☐ ☐ ☐

10. I have non-Christian friends to whom I witness directly and indirectly. ☐ ☐ ☐ ☐

11. People have been encouraged because I was willing to guide and support to them over an extended period of time. ☐ ☐ ☐ ☐

13

Personal Notes

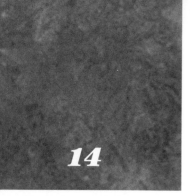

14

Personal Notes

		3	2	1	0
12.	I feel a deep concern for the spiritual welfare of Christians who are in a crisis.	☐	☐	☐	☐
13.	I would like to be involved in helping the homeless.	☐	☐	☐	☐
14.	I have a desire to proclaim truth that I have received from God with authority and conviction.	☐	☐	☐	☐
15.	I enjoy sharing God's promises from Scripture as a means of encouraging others.	☐	☐	☐	☐
16.	I go out of my way to meet new people and make them feel welcome and accepted.	☐	☐	☐	☐
17.	I feel comfortable spending time with non-Christians, never compromising my faith, but seeking to be a light to them.	☐	☐	☐	☐
18.	I find enjoyment working out the details necessary to organize people and resources for a more effective ministry.	☐	☐	☐	☐
19.	I enjoy being single and have little desire to become married.	☐	☐	☐	☐
20.	I like to do the small tasks that build up the Body of Christ.	☐	☐	☐	☐
21.	I enjoy inspiring and leading others for the sake of Christ's work.	☐	☐	☐	☐
22.	I have believed God can accomplish the impossible and have seen it happen in a tangible way.	☐	☐	☐	☐
23.	I have experienced an instant understanding of facts concerning people which I did not learn by natural means.	☐	☐	☐	☐
24.	I have had great dreams and aspirations which have turned into reality despite the unlikeliness of accomplishing them.	☐	☐	☐	☐

Frequently - 3   Sometimes - 2   Seldom - 1   Never - 0

15

Personal Notes

25. Serving others is high on my priority list, no matter what the task. ☐ ☐ ☐ ☐

26. When counseling a person, I can identify a problem correctly. ☐ ☐ ☐ ☐

27. I have seen people miraculously healed by my laying on of hands and prayer in Jesus' name. ☐ ☐ ☐ ☐

28. Though the idea scares me at times, I want to be in situations where the casting out of demons is necessary. ☐ ☐ ☐ ☐

29. I have an ability to see the "big picture" of a project and can coordinate others who only see various parts. ☐ ☐ ☐ ☐

30. I enjoy making anonymous donations when sharing my financial and material resources with others. ☐ ☐ ☐ ☐

31. I seem to have the ability to see how the Lord is working in people's lives, even in times of trial. ☐ ☐ ☐ ☐

32. I have opened my home and given shelter and food to those in need. ☐ ☐ ☐ ☐

33. I believe, without question, in evil spirits, and God has used me to command them to flee in Jesus' name. ☐ ☐ ☐ ☐

34. I am a strong believer that some individuals, including myself, should give more than a tithe (10%) of their income for the Lord's work. ☐ ☐ ☐ ☐

35. I enjoy living simply, even though I could easily afford a much more lavish lifestyle. ☐ ☐ ☐ ☐

36. Because of past results, people come to me to seek physical, emotional, or spiritual healing. ☐ ☐ ☐ ☐

37. I often sense a presence of good or evil in a person. ☐ ☐ ☐ ☐

Frequently - 3　　　Sometimes - 2　　　Seldom - 1　　　Never - 0

16

Personal Notes

38. People tend to call on me when help is needed for someone in distress.

☐ ☐ ☐ ☐

39. When I talk one-to-one with people, it frequently spurs them to take some positive action.

☐ ☐ ☐ ☐

40. At times I have a compelling urgency to stop what I am doing and pray for a person, a country, or a situation.

☐ ☐ ☐ ☐

41. I care deeply about those who haven't received Christ and feel God can use me to reach out to them.

☐ ☐ ☐ ☐

42. I believe demons can speak from inside a person and have witnessed this.

☐ ☐ ☐ ☐

43. I enjoy providing a haven for guests and do not feel imposed on, even by unexpected visitors.

☐ ☐ ☐ ☐

44. I have been instrumental in leading others to believe in Christ as their Savior.

☐ ☐ ☐ ☐

45. When in prayer, I have sensed an urging by the Holy Spirit to speak to God in a language I have never learned.

☐ ☐ ☐ ☐

46. I have the capacity to believe in the fulfillment of God's plans beyond normal or probable expectations.

☐ ☐ ☐ ☐

47. I have spoken an immediate message from God to His people in a language that I have never learned.

☐ ☐ ☐ ☐

48. I like to study the Bible in such a way that I can find personal application to what I am studying.

☐ ☐ ☐ ☐

49. I find myself working behind the scenes without the need for public recognition.

☐ ☐ ☐ ☐

Frequently - 3　　　**Sometimes - 2**　　　**Seldom - 1**　　　**Never - 0**

	3	2	1	0
50. I want to make myself available to be used for any type of duty or task in the church.	☐	☐	☐	☐
51. I am burdened to pray for someone at times and don't know why.	☐	☐	☐	☐
52. I have seen people delivered from satanic oppression or possession after I and others prayed for them.	☐	☐	☐	☐
53. When a person speaks in tongues, I get an idea about what God is saying.	☐	☐	☐	☐
54. I am concerned for people in other countries who need to hear the Gospel of Christ.	☐	☐	☐	☐
55. I feel I can witness to the poor people of my community because I can identify with them.	☐	☐	☐	☐
56. I seem to know when a situation is not right spiritually or morally.	☐	☐	☐	☐
57. When faced with a complex problem, I am able to isolate the heart of the problem and take steps to resolve it.	☐	☐	☐	☐
58. Because I am single, I have greater opportunity to serve the Body of Christ.	☐	☐	☐	☐
59. I seem to have a special ability to sense the mind of the Holy Spirit.	☐	☐	☐	☐
60. I have interpreted tongues with the result that the Body of Christ was edified, exhorted, or comforted.	☐	☐	☐	☐
61. I am willing to be available to those I encourage spiritually.	☐	☐	☐	☐
62. When I speak in tongues, I know I am speaking to God and not to man.	☐	☐	☐	☐
63. I feel called to pray for long periods of time.	☐	☐	☐	☐

17

Personal Notes

Frequently - 3   Sometimes - 2   Seldom - 1   Never - 0

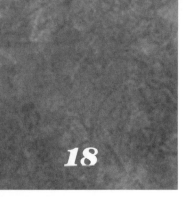

18

Personal Notes

	3	2	1	0
64. I can sense the Spirit of God actively helping me to pray.	☐	☐	☐	☐
65. God has revealed to me people's situations or problems.	☐	☐	☐	☐
66. I have delivered urgent messages from God's Word concerning the present or future.	☐	☐	☐	☐
67. I have a desire to see the spiritual and physical needs met of people who live in far away places.	☐	☐	☐	☐
68. I often rearrange my schedule to help others.	☐	☐	☐	☐
69. I exhibit confident trust in God despite apparent obstacles and increase the vision and trust of others in the Body.	☐	☐	☐	☐
70. I can work under pressure to accomplish established goals and objectives.	☐	☐	☐	☐
71. I want unreached people of other countries to have intercultural contacts and be included in a community of God's people.	☐	☐	☐	☐
72. During the discussion and sharing of a problem, I can share in a way that clarifies what is needed to resolve the problem.	☐	☐	☐	☐
73. I am always gathering up clothing, household items, and food for the needy.	☐	☐	☐	☐
74. When I speak in tongues, I believe it builds up the Body of Christ.	☐	☐	☐	☐
75. I am able to share the Gospel in a way that makes it clear and meaningful to non-believers.	☐	☐	☐	☐
76. I apply spiritual truth effectively in my own life.	☐	☐	☐	☐

Frequently - 3   Sometimes - 2   Seldom - 1   Never - 0

	3	2	1	0
77. Though not all are healed in Jesus' name when I pray for them, I still continue to pray for people who need physical healing.	☐	☐	☐	☐
78. My sharing of financial and material resources for Christian endeavors is one of the great joys of my Christian walk.	☐	☐	☐	☐
79. Preparing meals or helping those less fortunate gives me great satisfaction and pleasure.	☐	☐	☐	☐
80. After I pray for people, God has brought about supernatural changes in their lives or circumstances.	☐	☐	☐	☐
81. Though it may be difficult, I would be very willing to take charge in a situation where someone in the church needs to be disciplined.	☐	☐	☐	☐
82. I view my home as a place of ministry.	☐	☐	☐	☐
83. I believe God works through me to perform powerful acts.	☐	☐	☐	☐
84. I am not frustrated by unfulfilled sexual impulses.	☐	☐	☐	☐
85. I have gained spiritual insight from the Scriptures concerning people and issues which make me want to speak out.	☐	☐	☐	☐
86. I seem to be able to sense the power of God's presence when praying for healing, sometimes through a sense of warmth, energy or tingling.	☐	☐	☐	☐
87. The long-term spiritual welfare of family, friends, and acquaintances is very important to me.	☐	☐	☐	☐
88. Because I am single, I believe I have opportunities to accomplish more for the Lord.	☐	☐	☐	☐

19

Personal Notes

Frequently - 3   Sometimes - 2   Seldom - 1   Never - 0

20

Personal Notes

STEP 1 – continued	3	2	1	0
89. I enjoy communicating biblical truth to others and seeing growth in their knowledge of the Christian faith.	☐	☐	☐	☐
90. I can distinguish between works of the flesh and fruit of the Spirit.	☐	☐	☐	☐
91. Others tell me they gain new insight into biblical truth as a result of my leading a Bible study.	☐	☐	☐	☐
92. I have suddenly known things that are needed by a person or group, though I didn't know how I came to know these things.	☐	☐	☐	☐
93. I feel God has spoken to me through the Spirit, providing direction and spiritual insight for myself, my family, or a group of believers.	☐	☐	☐	☐
94. I openly share my material possessions with others when they are in need (i.e. tools, car, etc.).	☐	☐	☐	☐
95. I enjoy working on task-oriented projects rather than person-centered or one-to-one projects.	☐	☐	☐	☐
96. When I speak in tongues, it is to glorify God and not for my own gratification.	☐	☐	☐	☐
97. I want God to use me to defeat Satan by casting out demons and evil spirits in Jesus' name.	☐	☐	☐	☐
98. I have a tendency to make others feel warm, wanted, welcomed, and accepted.	☐	☐	☐	☐
99. I have prayed I may interpret if someone begins speaking in tongues.	☐	☐	☐	☐
100. I enjoy providing oversight and direction for a group's follow-through on its spiritual goals and objectives.	☐	☐	☐	☐

Frequently - 3   **Sometimes - 2**   **Seldom - 1**   **Never - 0**

Discovering Your Ministry Identity

21

Personal Notes

101. I have contributed spiritual insight to the solution of conflicts or problems within the Body of Christ. ☐ ☐ ☐ ☐

102. People are often amazed at my wisdom, even if I may not have much academic training. ☐ ☐ ☐ ☐

103. I enjoy short-term tasks rather than long-term projects. ☐ ☐ ☐ ☐

104. Impossible situations change when I pray for the Lord's intervention. ☐ ☐ ☐ ☐

105. I feel deep empathy for people who are suffering and translate my feelings into action. ☐ ☐ ☐ ☐

106. I believe material possessions are not important for me to feel successful and happy. ☐ ☐ ☐ ☐

107. People have told me I have helped them grow spiritually. ☐ ☐ ☐ ☐

108. Others in the church have confirmed I can "sense" the motives of a person's heart. ☐ ☐ ☐ ☐

109. People seek me out when they need guidance for planning and managing a particular task related to ministry. ☐ ☐ ☐ ☐

110. I am able to speak enthusiastically and clearly about doctrinal truth, providing comfort, guidance, warning, or encouragement. ☐ ☐ ☐ ☐

111. I feel confident, when I give sacrificially, the Lord will provide for my needs. ☐ ☐ ☐ ☐

112. I am content as a single person and am certain that is what the Lord wants for me at this time in my life. ☐ ☐ ☐ ☐

113. I desire to see God bring physical, emotional or spiritual help to people and am willing to be His hands. ☐ ☐ ☐ ☐

Frequently - 3   Sometimes - 2   Seldom - 1   Never - 0

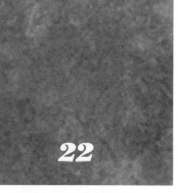

22

Personal Notes

		3	2	1	0
114.	After praying for hurting people, I can identify with them and can extraordinarily sense their grief.	☐	☐	☐	☐
115.	I have shared biblical truth with others in a way they have found meaningful and helpful.	☐	☐	☐	☐
116.	I receive great joy and peace discipling others in their spiritual walk.	☐	☐	☐	☐
117.	I have interpreted tongues in a way that seemed to bless others.	☐	☐	☐	☐
118.	I confidently expect God to respond to situations I have committed to Him in prayer.	☐	☐	☐	☐
119.	Teaching others the biblical truths I have learned through Bible study is very satisfying to me.	☐	☐	☐	☐
120.	Others say they admire me for my ability to live a simple lifestyle.	☐	☐	☐	☐
121.	I have experienced God urging me to step out and face unbeatable odds, and I know, through Him, positive change will occur.	☐	☐	☐	☐
122.	Unlike the rich young ruler (Matt. 19), I feel confident, if asked, I could willingly sell all I own and become poor to advance the Kingdom of God.	☐	☐	☐	☐
123.	I have interpreted tongues in such a way that the message appeared to be directly from God.	☐	☐	☐	☐
124.	People seem to look to me for leadership when I am in a group.	☐	☐	☐	☐
125.	I have witnessed God's performance of miracles in my life.	☐	☐	☐	☐

Frequently - 3   Sometimes - 2   Seldom - 1   Never - 0

Heights Spiritual Gifts
Summary Chart

1. In the chart below, enter the numerical value of each of your responses next to the number corresponding to the statement from the questionnaire.

Frequently - 3   **Sometimes - 2**   **Seldom - 1**   **Never - 0**

2. Add up the five numbers you have recorded in each row and place the sum in the "Total" column.

Gift ID No.	Statement Numbers and Value of Answers					Total	Spiritual Gift
1	1.	6.	23.	65.	92.		Word of Knowledge
2	2.	3.	54.	67.	71.		Missionary
3	26.	37.	56.	90.	108.		Discerning of Spirits
4	4.	30.	34.	78.	111.		Giving
5	5.	49.	68.	94.	103.		Helps
6	27.	36.	77.	86.	113.		Healing
7	7.	20.	25.	50.	95.		Service
8	8.	12.	15.	31.	39.		Exhortation
9	9.	21.	81.	100.	124.		Leadership
10	10.	17.	41.	44.	75.		Evangelism
11	11.	61.	87.	107.	116.		Pastoring
12	28.	33.	42.	52.	97.		Exorcism
13	13.	38.	73.	79.	105.		Mercy
14	14.	66.	85.	93.	110.		Prophecy
15	35.	55.	106.	120.	122.		Voluntary Poverty
16	16.	32.	43.	82.	98.		Hospitality
17	40.	51.	63.	64.	114.		Intercession
18	18.	29.	57.	70.	109.		Administration
19	45.	47.	62.	74.	96.		Tongues
20	48.	89.	91.	115.	119.		Teaching
21	53.	60.	99.	117.	123.		Interpretation
22	22.	24.	46.	69.	118.		Faith
23	19.	58.	84.	88.	112.		Celibacy
24	59.	72.	76.	101.	102.		Word of Wisdom
25	80.	83.	104.	121.	125.		Miracles

Summary Note: To determine the accuracy of your top six scores, go to Appendix A (page 41) and study the strengths and liabilities for each of your top six. Also take note of the results on page 25. Then order the top four gifts according to your findings.

Here's What I Think of You!

Make three copies of this page. Then find three people who know you well and who are willing to be bluntly honest with you about who you really are. Give them each one copy of this page. Ask them to circle the 10 words or phrases on this page which best describe you. Secondly, ask them to rate the TOP THREE by putting a "1" by the one MOST like you, a "2" by the one next most like you, etc. They may pick words from any column up and down or across. Ask them to return this to you when completed. SAVE this original page as your final tally sheet.

This is what I think about _____ .

Shepherd	To care for/protect	People sensitivity
Orchestrator	To give direction	Vision/Team sense
Encourager	To motivate	Inspiration, practical application
Soul winner	New Christians	Strong conviction
Foundation builder	New churches	God-given authority
Doctrine developer	To impart understanding	Biblical facts
Understanding	To apply knowledge	God-given insight
Speak forth boldly	Proclaim truth	Scripture
God-given confidence	To step out	Unwavering boldness
Assisting	Frees others to use gifts	Helping
Planner	Organization	Providing the details
Need meeter	Help however, wherever	Practical support
Comforter	To show compassion	Tenderness in action
Liberally give away	To share resources	Sharing
Spiritual pulse	Distinguish good from evil	Spiritual analysis

Signed: _____

DIRECTIONS: Note the addition of the gifts in the far left column. Tally the 10 circled choices and the top three choices and compare with the gifts that relate to those choices made.

Personal Notes

Equipping Gifts...to equip others for their intended body life purpose

Gift	Key Word(s)	Desires	Leads By
Pastor	Shepherd	To care for/protect	People sensitivity
Leader	Orchestrator	To give direction	Vision/Team sense
Exhorter	Encourager	To motivate	Inspiration, practical application
Evangelist	Soul winner	New Christians	Strong conviction
Apostle	Foundation builder	New churches	God-given authority
Teacher	Doctrine developer	To impart understanding	Biblical facts
Wisdom	Understanding	To apply knowledge	God-given insight
Prophet	Speak forth boldly	Proclaim truth	Scripture
Faith	God-given confidence	To step out	Unwavering boldness

Supporting Gifts...action-oriented service that enables others

Gifts	Key Word(s)	Desires	Supports by
Helps	Assisting	Free others to use gifts	Helping
Administration	Planner	Organization	Providing the details
Service	Need meeter	Help however, wherever	Practical support
Mercy	Comforter	To show compassion	Tenderness in action
Giving	Liberally give away	To share resources	Sharing

Other Gifts

Gifts	Key Word(s)	Desires	Supports by
Discernment	Spiritual pulse	Distinguish good from evil	Spiritual analysis of Spirits

Summary Note: After completing the Gift Survey Summary (page 23), this exercise (pages 23-24), and Appendix A (pages 43-53), determine your top four gifts and list them on page 39.

Team Style Questionnaire

Name _____

INSTRUCTIONS: Put a 4 beside the choice that is most like you, a 3 beside the next most like you, 2 next and 1 beside the least likely response you would make within each group. Remember: this is about who you ARE, not who you want to be or think you should be.

1. I feel best about myself when I have:
   _____ a. seen the bright side of the situation
   _____ b. really taken charge and gotten something done
   _____ c. managed to stay out of a tempting situation that was not my job
   _____ d. been able to really "belong" to the group

2. When I meet a person I usually:
   _____ a. try to appreciate something about him or her in good taste
   _____ b. appear self-assured and strong
   _____ c. am proper and dignified in our relationship
   _____ d. am happy, open, and supportive in our relationship

3. When others describe me, they might say:
   _____ a. a tremendous encourager
   _____ b. a smart person who knows where he or she is going
   _____ c. a little distant and hard to move
   _____ d. easy to get along with but hard to pin down on issues

4. Other persons are more likely to do what I want if I:
   _____ a. don't push but remind them of the highest goals and possibilities
   _____ b. encourage them to agree with me by being dynamic
   _____ c. explain the reasons for doing something so they understand
   _____ d. make them feel at ease and comfortable

5. The main feeling others have about working with me is:
   _____ a. worthy and supportive
   _____ b. enthusiastic about joining in and providing guidance
   _____ c. that I will be fair and caring
   _____ d. that it is fun to be around me

6. If I were a disciple of Jesus, I would probably be:
   _____ a. like Andrew, supporting others who come to Christ
   _____ b. like Peter, ready to push forward and take risks
   _____ c. like Philip, careful and considerate of all the facts
   _____ d. like John, majoring in encouraging mutual love and respect

7. If I were going to have a motto, it would be:
   _____ a. do your best and others will notice and follow
   _____ b. if it is the right thing to do, do it, whatever the cost
   _____ c. don't forget to be faithful to those who have gone before
   _____ d. be a friend and others will believe in you

8. If there is a disagreement or conflict, I would:
   _____ a. recognize my part in the conflict and apologize
   _____ b. hold out for what I believe to be the right decision
   _____ c. offer my perspective on the important details, being factual
   _____ d. realize the group is more important than the issue: unify!

TO TOTAL: Add up all numbers in each category (a, b, c and d) and enter totals: a. _____   b. _____   c. _____   d. _____
See the next three pages for the interpretation of these scores.

Name _____

Instructions: Match the letters from the previous page with those on this page, and select the two highest scores/matching styles as your primary and secondary performance style. Read through the information on your style(s), and underline comments, spiritual gifts and liabilities you believe fit you. Then take a deeper look at your styles in the following two pages. Circle qualities that readily identify who you are.

Team Styles	Potential Spiritual Gifts	Potential Liabilities
a. Let Me Help You: defers to others freely, does not have to take charge, wants to serve others. Leads from **alongside** generally.	pastoring helps service mercy hospitality	• not directive enough at times • can be too nice: no clear answers emerge • may have a hard time saying "no"

What other styles do you need most? **b c d**

b. Let's Go: in charge, a pioneer, always moving the group ahead with new visions and new insights. Leads most effectively from the **front**.	leadership exhortation faith evangelism prophet	• may not listen well • challenges others inappropriately • challenges others without all the facts

What other styles do you need most? **a c d**

c. Let's Be Careful: insist on in-depth, detail work, must consider all the facts. Leads best from **alongside** or **front**.	administration knowledge teaching	• often critical of others, ideas • stays too close to outline • too rigid

What other styles do you need most? **a b d**

d. Let's Stay Together: team-oriented, tries to draw the group together and help it stay that way. Leads best from **alongside** or **front**.	pastoring exhortation wisdom mercy	• fearful of making decisions for the group • too careful of being firm or rigid • may be afraid to speak out in a group

What other styles do you need most? **a b c**

Note: It is not uncommon to choose your second highest score as your predominant Team Style after reviewing the above information and the detail sections found inside.

Reflect on the descriptions and do not be driven by the numbers alone.

Summary Note: List your top two team styles in the space provided on page 39.

TEAM STYLES A & B IN DETAIL

Team Issue	a."Let Me Help You"	b."Let's Go!"
Another Name	• alongside co-laborer	• visionary
Communication	• helping focus • purposeful encourager • alongside listener	• open, direct • invites potential • confront when needed
Planning Style	• discover direction with • set strategic course	• brainstorming • strategic • seek ownership/ vision
Vision	• let's discover together	• here's the vision...
Problem-solving/ Decision-making	• influence direction • seek unity of purpose • shared process	• set direction • ask hard questions • often intuitive
Risk-Taking	• prefers risking with others	• pushes new frontiers
Major Liability	• may not know when to stop helping and release	• less people-sensitive when vision-driven
Conflict Style	• "What's wrong?"	• often reactive
Potential Gifts	• pastor • hospitality • mercy • service/helps	• leader • evangelist • prophet • exhorter • faith

Team Issue	c."Let's Be Careful"	d."Let's Stay Together"
Another Name:	• detail analyst	• unity builder
Communication	• will not waste words • will be specific • may prefer written report to spoken	• relational focus • listener • pursues others
Planning Style	• concise • detailed	• group process • facilitating others
Vision	• do study to find vision	• discover unity in vision
Problem-solving/ Decision-making	• logical • analytical • cost-effective over vision	• unity is goal • often open-ended • committed to resolve
Risk-Taking	• based on facts • conservative	• careful not to offend • will seldom risk unity
Major Liability	• efficient over effective • form over substance	• commitment to unity • can overly dominate
Conflict Style	• may be controlling • "letter of the law"	• pulls back, non-directive • does not like conflict
Potential Gifts	• administrative • teaching • knowledge	• pastoring • mercy • exhortation • wisdom

Adapted and expanded from Glenn Parker, Team Players and Teambuilding.

29

Personal Notes

What Is Your Ministry Burden Or Passion?

Name _____

What is your vision or heart to develop a ministry or service to meet the needs of either Christians or non-Christians? Money is not an object! Please offer your own creative thoughts. What would you be willing to invest in personally?

PART A: If You Could Create Your Own Ministry/Serving Area...

1. If I were to create a new ministry, group, or serving area it would be

_____

_____

2. The reason I believe this ministry or group is needed is because

_____

_____

3. How many people would need to be involved in this project, and in what roles would they be?

_____

_____

4. If I were to play a part in this ministry, my role would be

_____

_____

PART B: In Whom or What are You Willing to Invest Your Life?

Some people more clearly understand an area of burden or passion that God has placed in their lives by considering the burdens or passions of others. As you consider these areas, see if you can identify an activity, a group of people, or a geographical location where you have some heart-felt desires where you could invest your life.

- **Specific activity?** ...teaching, feeding the poor, hospital visits, one-to-one discipling...
- **Specific group of people?** ...blue collar workers, single moms, the elderly, high schoolers...
- **Specific location?** ...Russia, Mexico City, Boston, your hometown, your neighbors...

As you consider possibilities, remember that the goal is not just to come up with a "good idea." Rather, it is to discover or affirm a passion or burden area where you could or already are investing your life.

Summary Note: After identifying one or two areas of your potential ministry burdens or passions, please note those in the space provided on page 39.

Your Vital Values
The Real Non-Negotiables in Your Life

Value Defined: **That which is highly important or vital to me. The things I value are those which define the way I live my life, share in relationships, or fulfill my work obligations. That which I highly value will be revealed significantly in the way I live.**

SECTION A: My Vital Values Work, Lifestyle, and Relationships

Rate each of the following with a score from 5 to 1 with 5 being very significant and 1 being unimportant. *Further instructions will be given at the end.*

In my work, lifestyle, and relationships, I value:

____ 1. **Aesthetics**: Studying or appreciating the beauty of things, ideas, etc.

____ 2. **Affiliation**: Being part of a group, organization, or team, where I am accepted as a member.

____ 3. **Artistic Expression**: The opportunity to create various works of art that have aesthetic value.

____ 4. **Challenges**: The opportunity to stretch myself with new, unique, or difficult tasks or issues that present some form of challenge.

____ 5. **Change and Variety**: Experiences at work or play that allow for a great deal of newness, change, or many different options.

____ 6. **Competence**: The opportunity to work in an area(s) where I have particular strength or expertise and will be able to excel.

____ 7. **Competition**: Activities which pit my abilities against others where there are clear win and lose outcomes.

____ 8. **Creative Expression**: The opportunity to express my ideas, reactions, or observations by spoken word, in writing, or in another artistic form.

____ 9. **Decision Making — top level**: Being in a position to lead teams to develop the course of action or direction for a group, team, organization, or company.

____ 10. **Decision Making — mid level**: With clear authority in place over me, the opportunity to set a course of action or policy direction for a group within a larger organization or company.

____ 11. **Decision Making — policy only**: Being in a position of establishing policy upon which other people will carry through in their respective group or organization.

____ 12. **Energy**: Being in situations which demand high energy level and enthusiasm.

____ 13. **Equipping/Training**: The opportunity to help others through a process to develop certain skills or carry out new responsibilities in an effective way.

____ 14. **Excitement**: The opportunity to participate in adventurous, fun, and captivating experiences on an ongoing basis.

____ 15. **Fast Pace**: Experiencing a rapid pace of action or a lot of activity on a regular basis.

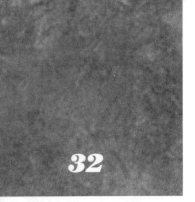

16. Feelings: The opportunity to be warm, sympathetic and encouraging in relationships, to emphasize the emotional part of who we are as people.

17. Friendliness: Being a friendly person in group situations, always positive and upbeat.

18. Friendship: The opportunity to develop close personal relationships as a result of my work, volunteer activities, or life situation.

19. Help Society: Actively contribute to the betterment of the world or community in which I live.

20. Help Others: The opportunity to provide service or assistance to others in a practical way, either individually or with a group.

21. High Earnings: Making a significant amount of money that allows me to live a financially secure life.

22. Independence: The opportunity to determine the nature of my work or lifestyle without significant direction from others; the freedom to set my own course rather than merely following orders.

23. Influence People: The opportunity to affect others to change an attitude or to move them toward a certain course of action.

24. Knowledge: Spending a great amount of time and focus in the pursuit of knowledge, truth, and understanding.

25. Leadership: The opportunity to lead others on a specific mission or process by directing, influencing, and motivating them.

26. Leisure: Having enough time to relax or participate in many activities which fulfill my need for relaxation.

27. Listening: Giving high priority for others to share their joys, needs, and struggles with me.

28. Location: The opportunity to live in the same location, one that fits my lifestyle and needs, for an extended period of time.

29. Meetings: Being in groups that are meeting for a defined purpose and a defined period of time to fulfill certain objectives.

30. Moral Fulfillment: Feeling that my work contributes to a set of moral standards to which I and my organization are committed.

31. Mental Stimulation: The opportunity to do work which requires constant or consistent use of my mind. I greatly value intellectual challenge.

32. Options: Having as many options as possible available to me in my life and work.

33. Persuasion: The opportunity to influence or convince others about a vision, plan, or product.

34. Physical Activity: The opportunity to be physically active on a regular basis in my work or lifestyle.

35. Pioneering: Exploring new situations or discovering new ways to do things. Adventure!

36. Position: Holding a job or position which brings me the respect of others.

37. Power and Authority: The opportunity to oversee or direct the activities, direction, and rewards of my organization, team, or group.

38. Precision: The opportunity to be involved in work or an activity which requires a great deal of accuracy.

39. Pressure: Enjoying situations where deadlines or critical analysis by others is a priority of the task at hand.

40. Privacy: The opportunity to work or relax in a setting where I am alone and uninterrupted for long periods of time.

41. Public Contact: Having consistent, ongoing interaction with people.

42. Recognition: The opportunity to receive affirmation or reward for things I have said or done.

43. Reliability: The opportunity to show others I am someone who will follow through in a variety of situations.

44. Responsibility: Having primary responsibility for people or projects in such a way that I can show myself to be capable and trustworthy.

45. Security (Financial): Being assured of my job and its financial rewards over an extended period of time.

46. Security (Relational): Being comfortable and assured of the long term nature of commitment in relationships.

47. Spontaneity: The opportunity for unplanned events, unstructured time, and surprises.

48. Stability: Having a work situation or lifestyle which is largely predictable and not likely to change significantly over an extended period of time.

49. Structure: Giving high priority to orderliness, details, and preplanned activities.

50. Teamwork: The opportunity to work with a team or group on a regular basis and value the relationships on the team.

51. Team Unity: Experiencing ongoing harmony and oneness in our group, no matter what the cost.

52. Technical or Scientific Knowledge: The opportunity to work in a scientific or research area that strives for technical expertise or seeks to advance certain disciplines.

53. Time Freedom: Having a work routine that I can pursue at my own schedule—that is, no defined work hours are required.

54. Tranquility: The opportunity to have a work setting or lifestyle that has few pressures or changes along the way.

SECTION A: Summary

In the blanks below, rank your top five (#5) values, in order of priority. Your most important value would be #1, second highest #2, and so on.

1. _____

2. _____

3. _____

4. _____

5. _____

In the blanks below, rank your lowest-rated (#1) values. Your lowest value of all would be #1, second lowest #2, and so on.

1. _____

2. _____

3. _____

4. _____

5. _____

Summary Note: List your three highest and three lowest values on page 40.

SECTION B: Vital Values in Training Others

Rate each of the following topics with a score from 5 being very significant to 1 being unimportant. *(For example, #5 for Authoritative Leadership, #1 for Community, #3 for Creativity, etc.).*

In training, leading, or equipping others, I value:

____ **Community**: It is important to share deeper feelings and needs.

____ **Creativity**: New ideas and projects are important to affirm, giving individuals the opportunity to discover their place to serve.

____ **Democratic Process**: Discussion and consensus is important on important decisions.

____ **Diversity**: It is more important to allow different attitudes or actions than just the plan already laid out.

____ **Individuality**: It is important each team member be able to affirm their individuality, even if it affects team unity.

____ **Integrity**: Having unquestioned character and principles is very important.

____ **Participation of Others**: Everyone must have the chance to fulfill one or more roles in a specific ministry or on a team.

____ **Strength**: The leader's decisions are to be followed.

____ **Trust**: It is important to believe in others, and to trust them with specific ministry responsibilities.

____ **Vision**: Vision and direction must be clear enough to be understood and followed.

SECTION B: Summary

In the blanks below, list your top three (#3) Training Values, in order of their importance. Your most important value would be #1, second highest #2, and so on.

1. _____

2. _____

3. _____

In the blanks below, list your bottom three Training Values for you.

1. _____

2. _____

3. _____

Summary Note: List your three highest and three lowest training values in the space provided on page 40.

Section A was adapted and expanded from an assessment tool found in "Personal Assessment and Development" by the Navigator's Career Development Team, Colorado Springs, CO.

SECTION C: Vital Values in Decision Making

As in Section B, rate each of the following topics with a score from 5 being very significant to 1 being unimportant. You may use the same priority number no more than three times (i.e. no more than three #1s, etc.). All five priority numbers #5, #4, #3, #2, and #1 must be used at least once.

In Decision-Making, other than *prayer* and *the Bible*, I value:

____ **Advice**: The encouragement or counsel I receive from people I respect or trust.

____ **Emotions**: My feelings, my subjective sense.

____ **Experience**: My own set of sensory experiences give me clear answers—what I have already seen, heard, felt, tasted, or smelled in my life.

____ **Faith**: My depth of conviction about the situation, person, or facts.

____ **Honor**: Making certain the needs and concerns of others are given top priority.

____ **Intuition**: My internal sense, my "gut" reaction, which, at times, will not be based on facts or data.

____ **Logic**: If I think it through, step by step, I will come to the reasonable, sensible conclusions.

____ **Other**: _____
_____
_____
_____

SECTION C: Summary

In the blanks below, list your top two Decision Making Values, in order of priority.

1. _____

2. _____

In the blanks below, list your bottom two Decision Making Values, in order of priority.

1. _____

2. _____

Summary Note: List your two highest and two lowest decision-making values in the space provided on page 40.

SECTION D: Vital Values in a Team Ministry Setting

Rank the following words in order of importance to you. For example, unity may be highest at *#4*, orderliness next at *#3*, adventure *#2*, and support as the lowest *#1*).

In working together on a Ministry Team, I value:

____ **Unity**: Harmony in relationships.

____ **Support**: Helping one another.

____ **Orderliness**: Clear purpose and procedures.

____ **Adventure**: New opportunities and directions.

Highest Rated: _____

Why did you rate your top choice so highly?

_____

_____

Summary Note: List your two highest and two lowest values in the space provided on page 40.

SECTION E: Personal Summary *(Optional)*

Write a brief summary of your Vital Values. These exercises provide a simple overview of who you are by asking you to determine what is important to you in different parts of your life. Write 10 sentences that describe your Vital Values to someone who wants to know more about who you are and what is important to you.

1. _____

2. _____

3. _____

4. _____

5. _____

6. _____

7. _____

8. _____

9. _____

10. _____

Primary Functions of Leadership

What you do best is defined by your Ministry Identity...

Rate yourself on each of the following.

5 = That's me, 3 = Somewhat like me, 1 = Not me at all

Primary Functions of Leadership

When I am leading or am a part of a team...

1. _____ I keep the team on track with its stated priorities and values.

2. _____ I build partnerships for the tasks at hand, giving priority to relationships in the process.

3. _____ I listen for ministry burdens or passions, team unity issues or problems.

4. _____ I tend to clarify the vision/direction and set the course.

5. _____ I invest in others and release them to play their God-designed role.

6. _____ I desire carefulness in plans and performance.

7. _____ I focus on relational quality control rather than task quality control.

8. _____ I tend to ask questions long before giving answers.

9. _____ I may or may not originate the vision, but I often end up communicating it.

10. _____ I provide or direct others to needed training to help fulfill their ministry identity.

11. _____ I manage process and details in administration, planning and controlling.

12. _____ I provide a context of belonging for others in the group or team.

13. _____ I tend to encourage two-way communication.

14. _____ I draw vision and people together in a way that produces fruit in carrying out the vision.

15. _____ I prepare, mend, and mentor others to fulfill their God-designed purpose.

16. _____ I may not initiate vision, but I establish signposts to keep us on track.

17. _____ I intentionally work to build unity on the team.

18. _____ I cause people to believe that they are heard when expressing vision or concerns.

19. _____ I enable others to believe that they can contribute to fulfilling the vision.

20. _____ I am able to encourage the best in others and validate them to play their parts.

Summary Note: Tally your scores at right then list your results on the bottom of page 40.

Scoring:

Values Keeper
1. _____
6. _____
11. _____
16. _____
_____ Total

Team Builder
2. _____
7. _____
12. _____
17. _____
_____ Total

Active Listener
3. _____
8. _____
13. _____
18. _____
_____ Total

Vision Sharer
4. _____
9. _____
14. _____
19. _____
_____ Total

Equipping Releaser
5. _____
10. _____
15. _____
20. _____
_____ Total

Teamshredding Attitudes

Which of these attitudes may be areas where you could actually "tear the fabric" of your group or team?

1. **Denial:** I do not see the problem, so it is not there.

2. **Blind Spots and Shortcuts:** What I do not like cannot be important.

3. **Self Interest:** Look out for number one.

4. **Mind Reading:** People should know without being told.

5. **Blame:** It has to be somebody's fault.

6. **Too Nice:** Avoid conflict at all cost.

7. **Perfection:** If it is not perfect, it is nothing.

8. **Fairness:** I want you to be "fairer" with me than anybody else.
   (i.e. I want you to show me special favor.)

9. **Excuses:** There is a good reason for this.

10. **I Am Right:** There is a right way and a wrong way—and mine is right.

Teamshredder   #1 _____   #2 _____   #3 _____

Adapted from <u>Sacred Bull</u>, by Bernstein and Rozen (NY: Wiley & Sons)

Focusing Your Ministry Identity

CONSOLIDATE YOUR CORE COMPONENTS

Now that you have completed the individual exercises, you are ready to summarize your findings. As you focus your ministry identity, take note of each of the categories listed on pages 39 and 40 and make certain that you accurately identified, to the best of your ability at this time, who you are. If you missed filling in a category, see the bottom of this page for the appropriate pages for each one. This summary may give you a clearer sense of your true ministry identity, and it will be an invaluable tool for sharing with others on your team or in your group. How you fit with others on a team may also become clearer through this process.

Your results come from the following pages:
Spiritual Gifts	(pages 23, 25, 41)
Team Styles	(pages 27-29)
Ministry Burden or Passion	(page 30)
Your Vital Values	(pages 33-36)
Principle Priorities	(page 37)

POTENTIAL SPIRITUAL GIFTS: The Supernatural How

1. _____

2. _____

3. _____

4. _____

TEAM STYLES: How I Function on a Team

1. _____

2. _____

BURDENS/PASSIONS: The Supernatural Who, What, or Where

1. _____

2. _____
(Add a second one if you have one.)

YOUR VITAL VALUES

Vital Values: **Discovering that which I highly value reveals a great deal about how I live, work, and relate to others.**

HIGH VALUES:	**LOW VALUES:**
A: Work/Lifestyle	**A: Work/Lifestyle**
1._____	1._____
2._____	2._____
3._____	3._____
4._____	4._____
5._____	5._____
B: Training	**B: Training**
1._____	1._____
2._____	2._____
3._____	3._____
C: Decision Making	**C: Decision Making**
1._____	1._____
2._____	2._____
D: Team	**D: Team**
1._____	1._____
2._____	2._____

PRINCIPLE PRIORITIES: My Strengths and Who I Need

Top 2	Needy 2
5._____	1._____
4._____	2._____

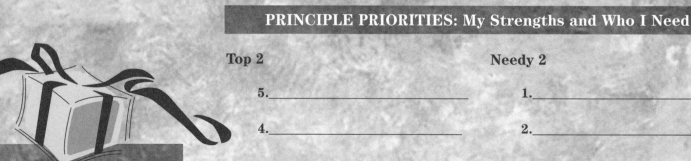

Appendix A:

Spiritual Gift Definitions & Characteristics

Take the gifts which made up your six highest scores from the gifts survey and note the characteristics and liabilities of each of those gifts. You may end up changing the order of those top six when you compare and contrast how much each is really who you are. After working through the six gifts, list what you now believe to be your top four gifts. Don't just believe the scores... take serious stock of what your gifts truly are!

MY TOP SIX GIFTS FROM THE HEIGHTS GIFTS SURVEY

(list only one gift per line)

1. _____

2. _____

3. _____

4. _____

5. _____

6. _____

AFTER STUDY, THESE ARE MY TOP FOUR GIFTS

(list in order of strength)

1. _____

2. _____

3. _____

4. _____

Special Notes:

- *Spiritual gifts do not have liabilities. People do have liabilities when trying to exercise certain gifts on their own strength.*

- *To do a deeper scripture study on spiritual gifts, please use one of Paul Ford's other workbooks called <u>Getting Your Gifts in Gear</u>.*

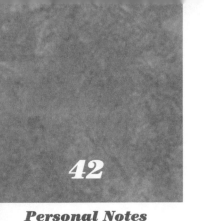

Supporting Spiritual Gifts

These gifts tend to be more action-oriented in function. Such gifts often work behind the scenes, and people with these gifts are usually extremely faithful in their service.

Administration	Mercy
Giving	Service
Helps	

ADMINISTRATION:

Definition: **The supernatural ability to provide organization for the goals of the body of Christ by designing and carrying out an efficient plan of action.**

Gift Characteristics:

1. Like a navigator on ship, they plot the course, or, like a musical conductor, they put together all the parts of the music for the orchestra to play.
2. Carry vision into reality by putting the details into a plan of action.
3. Tend to be more task- and detail-centered than people-centered.
4. Focus on the details of the vision, part by part, rather than the "big picture."
5. Usually are implementors of vision rather than imparters of vision.
6. Careful planners.

Gift Liabilities:

1. May view people as "task completers" rather than people.
2. May be unresponsive to suggestions and changes in plans they have made.
3. May not communicate explanations, praise or specifics of the process to team members.
4. May rely on their well-organized plans rather than the Spirit and prayer.
5. May be too careful and block the overall vision with their many specific details.
6. May show favoritism to those who seem more loyal.

GIVING

Definition: **The supernatural ability to give freely, cheerfully, and sacrificially of one's money or possessions for the sake of Christ and His body.**

Gift Characteristics:

1. Freely gives out of whatever resources are available.
2. Sees money and possessions as tools to serve God, and set those resources aside for special use.
3. Their giving is often quiet and confidential – no fanfare is desired.
4. Shows strong interest and support in the people and causes they support.
5. Gives liberally to the churches, missions, and other causes which advance the Kingdom of God.

Gift Liabilities:

1. Giver's own family may suffer because too much has been given away!
2. May be critical of how others spend their money.
3. May pressure or expect others to give like they do.
4. May be misled into giving to causes which do not further the cause of Christ.
5. May give without holding the recipient accountable.

HELPS:

Definition: **The supernatural ability to unselfishly meet the needs of others, freeing them to exercise their spiritual gift(s).**

Gift Characteristics:

1. Sees what needs to be done in assisting others and desires to do it.
2. Typically unselfish because of the strong desire to help.
3. Assists others in specific ministries.
4. Finds great joy in freeing others from responsibilities so that they can share their gifts.
5. Rejoices in the fruitfulness of others.

Gift Liabilities:

1. May have difficulty saying "no" when asked to help, even when they need to say "no."
2. May easily become overextended physically and/or emotionally.
3. May feel taken for granted if not affirmed in their support role.
4. May take too much ownership in helping others or in not letting others help.
5. May seek to be too helpful and end up getting in the way unintentionally.
6. May neglect their own needs and their family's/close friend's needs to help others.

MERCY

Definition: **The supernatural ability to show great empathy and compassion for those who suffer physically, emotionally, or spiritually, and to assist them.**

Gift Characteristics:

1. Shows sincere kindness and compassion in their lifestyle.
2. Reveals significant "love in action."
3. Often are drawn to those who may be outcasts or considered as outsiders.
4. Able to patiently stay alongside someone who is ill.
5. Attempts to relieve the source of people's suffering.
6. Effective in ministering to those who are terminally ill.
7. Cheerfully aids the unloved, often without recognition.

Gift Liabilities:

1. May be too protective of the person(s) for whom they care.
2. Without realizing it, may identify too strongly with someone hurting or ill.
3. May base decisions on emotion rather than reason.
4. May condemn and withdraw from people who appear insensitive to others.
5. May have great difficulty saying "no" to a need even when they should.

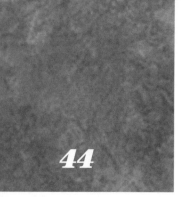

SERVICE

Definition: **The supernatural ability to identify unmet needs in the Body of Christ and beyond, and to use whatever resources necessary to practically meet those needs.**

Gift Characteristics:

1. Resourceful in meeting needs.
2. Offers practical solutions.
3. Loves to serve, often without receiving any public affirmation. Doing the task is enough!
4. Will often change their schedule to serve others.
5. Able to see needs arising before others see them.

Gift Liabilities:

1. May neglect responsibilities at home to serve others.
2. May exclude others from helping by their own drive to serve.
3. May wear out physically because of their difficulty with saying "no."
4. May find self-esteem needs in doing things for others rather than accepting themselves for who they are.
5. May over-commit and then feel abused.
6. May go around proper authority to get tasks done.
7. May use the gift inappropriately to gain acceptance and appreciation of others.

Equipping Spiritual Gifts

Equipping Spiritual Gifts are more verbal in function. Their role in the Body of Christ is to prepare and release others for service. People with these gifts often function effectively either up front in leading others or coming alongside others to encourage them. It should be noted that many alongside equippers are not comfortable in an up front role.

Apostle	**Leadership**
Exhortation	**Pastoring**
Evangelism	**Prophet**
Faith	**Teaching**

Some would include: Wisdom/Word of Wisdom

APOSTLE

Definition: **With full authority from God, the supernatural ability to build spiritual foundations and plant new churches in expanding the ministry and scope of the Church.**

Gift Characteristics:

1. Primary tasks: to preach to the unsaved, to plant churches, to equip the saints for the work of ministry, and to do each with authority over a broad area or country.
2. Someone who starts new churches or ministries over a broad spectrum where many are converted in the process. It is more than just a pioneer who starts new things.
3. Builds spiritual foundations in which others grow – note Paul as an "expert builder" (1 Corinthians 3:10). Functions as foundation builder for God's household (Ephesians 2:20).
4. Literally means "one sent on a mission." Implies travel to many places.
5. Functions as an authority over a group or region of churches, both by spoken and written word, and provides oversight for many younger leaders.
6. Note: very, very few will have this gift (author has seen fewer than ten over his 20 years in ministry). Some even believe this gift is no longer functioning.

Gift Liabilities:

1. May experience problems with power and control if they try to practice this gift in the flesh.
2. May exhibit an inappropriate authoritarian attitude when dealing with others.
3. May want to move on to the next project before the present one has a sufficient foundation.

EXHORTATION

Definition: **The supernatural ability to encourage, comfort, challenge or rebuke others to action in such a way that they respond.**

Gift Characteristics:

1. Encourages and motivates others to practical application of specific Biblical truths.
2. Motivates people to apply Scripture, not just learn it.
3. Tells others the truth about themselves with great encouragement and understanding.
4. Encourages people to discover what they can become and sets up opportunities for them to fulfill those possibilities.
5. Committed to offering specific, practical guidance for others' spiritual growth.
6. May take the form of rebuke, though people will still feel helped by such an approach.
7. Often more effective in short-term encouragement than long-term counseling or support.

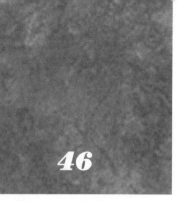

Gift Liabilities:

1. May struggle with follow-through with an individual or project because they want to move on and exhort someone else.
2. May offer "quick fixes" and appear insensitive to longer term needs.
3. May jump to conclusions before listening to the whole story.
4. May offer too direct or harsh counsel at one extreme or be insensitive to the real need at the other extreme.
5. May become more vision-centered than person-centered because of desire for the person to take practical steps.

EVANGELISM

Definition: **The supernatural ability to share the Gospel with unbelievers in such a way that people respond and became followers of Jesus Christ.**

Gift Characteristics:

1. Has an ongoing desire to share the Good News with many people!
2. Able to clearly present the message of salvation to non-Christians.
3. Shares the Gospel in such a way that people respond by accepting Christ.
4. Often most effective in one type of evangelistic effort and not necessarily others: i.e. one-to-one, open air preaching, small group settings, etc.
5. Wants others to share their faith effectively and win the world for Jesus Christ!
6. Understands with passion that God desires all people to be saved.

Gift Liabilities:

1. May become obnoxious if they rely on their own strength and insight to convert people.
2. May become prideful over the number of people they lead to Christ.
3. May motivate by guilt when encouraging others to share their faith.
4. May be very narrow in their evangelistic focus and discount the gifts of others.
5. May see people as "targets" and not as people with needs.
6. Often are seen as overly directive by others, Christian or non-Christian.

FAITH

Definition: **The supernatural ability to trust God with extra-ordinary confidence, knowing that He will work out His purposes in every situation.**

Gift Characteristics:

1. Able to trust God to work in supernatural ways.
2. Confident that situations will ultimately change for the glory of God, even when the situation seems impossible.
3. Willing to carry out God's will in the midst of enormous difficulties or barriers.
4. Willing to yield to God's will rather than question or waver because of circumstances.
5. Often moves out in faith when others are unwilling.

Gift Liabilities:

1. May exercise faith without love.
2. May be impatient when others are more timid or careful.
3. Because of blind faith, may set up self or others for failure.
4. May be stubborn and unyielding instead of being willing to listen to counsel.
5. May see concern about their vision as a criticism of God and a hindrance to His work rather than fair questioning.

LEADERSHIP

Definition: **The supernatural ability to provide overall vision for the Body of Christ and provide direction for others in such a way that they willingly follow and work together.**

Gift Characteristics:

1. If an administrator puts the pieces of music together, then the leader is the conductor of the orchestra, involving each person meaningfully in the "music," the process.
2. Provides vision and direction for the overall process, the "big picture."
3. The only gift that appears able to effectively deal with both the vision and the people who will carry out the vision.
4. Often are able to see the final results of a major undertaking in advance.
5. Shares vision effectively with others and is able to involve many people in the process of completing the task.
6. Appears in charge, even if not identified as the official leader.
7. The primary fruit: people follow.

Gift Liabilities:

1. Value to the organization may be lost if they get too involved with the details of the vision.
2. May become insensitive to individuals carrying out details of the vision because of focus on the big picture.
3. May become overly dominant or demanding if not sensitive to the Spirit.
4. May become prideful of their position or power.
5. May forget that they do not have all the details of the vision. That is, they may forget how much they need others to know and carry out the specifics of the vision.

PASTORING

Definition: **The supernatural ability to care for, feed, and protect the long term spiritual needs of individuals or groups in the Body of Christ.**

Gift Characteristics:

1. Greatly enjoys being with and ministering to people.
2. Provides care, spiritual nourishment, and protection for people over an extended period of time.
3. More person-centered than task-centered.
4. Derives great strength from encouraging and verbally supporting others.
5. Usually counsels and guides many people, whether or not they have had training to do such.

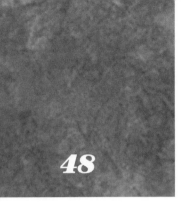

Gift Liabilities:

1. May have a difficult time saying "no" to others, often at the expense of their families/close friends and their own physical, emotional, and spiritual well-being.
2. May be indecisive because of the strong desire to be sensitive to others.
3. May be too protective of people and create a situation where people become too dependent on them.
4. May try to control people's decisions out of the desire to "protect" them.
5. May struggle with releasing people to grow beyond their pastoral control – more so than any other equipping gift.

PROPHET

Definition: **The supernatural ability to proclaim God's present and future truth in such a way that the hearers are moved to respond.**

Gift Characteristics:

1. Can be prophetic in either sense: challenges people by speaking about a future event (foretelling), or speaks forthrightly about present situations ("forthtelling").
2. Proclaims timely and urgent messages from God.
3. Response to gift may include repentance, strengthening, comfort or encouragement.
4. Proclaims the Scriptures with authority.
5. Often pleads the cause of God to His people and/or the world.
6. Prophets tend to forcefully challenge for decision to follow God's way.

Gift Liabilities:

1. May preach gloom, doom and despair that is not from God!
2. May experience pride and self-centeredness growing out of the authoritative nature of the gift.
3. May offer prophecy that disagrees with God's Word.
4. May communicate inaccurate foretelling.
5. Can be too blunt!

TEACHING

Definition: **The supernatural ability to clearly and accurately communicate the truths of the Bible in such a way that people learn.**

Gift Characteristics:

1. Has a strong desire and ability to communicate Biblical truth.
2. Is able to effectively instruct, reprove, correct and train using the Bible.
3. Is able to pull scriptural insights together in a clear and insightful way.
4. Communicates truth in such a way that people understand what is conveyed from God's Word.
5. Gives clear Biblical insight in dealing with life situations.

Gift Liabilities:

1. May appear to have all the answers, leaving little room for discussion.
2. May communicate too much information too quickly for the average learner.
3. If functioning on their own strength, may promote their own insight as Biblical and authoritative.
4. May become prideful of their own learning.
5. May be too content-focused with little or no people-focus.

WISDOM/WORD OF WISDOM

Definition: **The supernatural ability to offer pertinent spiritual counsel immediately in situations where such guidance is needed.**

Gift Characteristics:

1. Is able to apply spiritual knowledge in practical ways.
2. Has a supernatural understanding of situations in which they have no previous knowledge.
3. Offers practical, helpful solutions to problems – i.e. wise counsel.
4. When such gifted people speak, people learn to listen because of the consistently accurate and wise spiritual counsel that is offered.

Gift Liabilities:

1. May offer only human wisdom when functioning in their own strength, causing their counsel to be ineffective in the situation.
2. May force a personal view on others. This is a clear violation of this gift.
3. May become prideful when they realize people really listen when they speak!

Spiritual Gifts Growing Out of Prayer and Worship

As the name implies, these gifts commonly occur in the context of worship or in a setting where corporate prayer is taking place. They are often very dynamic in function, and may be interactive with the flow of worship. It should be noted here that not all Christians would include these gifts as active in our present age. They may only include the first, Discernment of Spirits, in their gifts list.

Discernment of Spirits	**Tongues**
Healing	**Interpretation of Tongues**
Miracles	**Word of Knowledge**
Some would include:	**Prophet**
	Wisdom/Word of Wisdom
	(Both found in
	last section)

DISCERNMENT OF SPIRITS

Definition: **The supernatural ability to determine whether a certain action has its source in God, man, or Satan.**

Gift Characteristics:

1. Is able to discern the source of a message or special word as being from God or Satan.
2. Is able to discern a person's spiritual motivation to be from God or Satan.
3. Has a profound sense of the spiritual realm, often sensing things in the spiritual realm that others simply do not experience.
4. Is often able to help others discover the spiritual source of their problems.

Gift Liabilities:

1. May unnecessarily become overzealous in hunting satanic heresy.
2. May be overly judgmental of others and their motives.
3. May be insensitive to the process needed for real change in a person's life when offering spiritual input on the source of problems or spiritual warfare.

HEALING

Definition: **The supernatural ability to miraculously restore health to an individual in the physical, emotional, or spiritual realms through a direct act of God.**

Gift Characteristics:

1. Believe that God can heal physical, emotional, and spiritual illness, and bear fruit to such happening.
2. Show a willingness to fail by praying for all who seek healing.
3. Some will have a gift of healing only in a specific area or two. Examples: healing headaches, lower back problems or emotional healing. When they pray for people in their special healing area, a high percentage of people are healed.
4. Believes God can heal but also believes that God may choose not to heal in certain circumstances.
5. As with miracles, may tie to the gift of faith.

Gift Liabilities:

1. May become prideful and seek personal gain through exercising this gift.
2. May exaggerate claims of healing to protect or further their reputation.
3. May feel personally responsible for someone not healed (i.e. see it as their fault rather than God's choice).
4. May overstep their area of healing ministry if God has prepared them to focus on one or two areas of healing.

MIRACLES (MIRACULOUS POWERS)

Definition: **The supernatural ability to transform the course of natural law in such a way that divine intervention is the only possible explanation.**

Gift Characteristics:

1. Experiences miraculous answers to prayer.
2. God will work through them to perform supernatural acts that are beyond the normal course of human and earthly activity.
3. The gift of faith sometimes works in tandem with this gift because of its supernatural ability to trust God to move mountains.
4. Others will confirm the miraculous events.

Gift Liabilities:

1. May claim to have performed a miracle, but circumstances do not verify that it happened.
2. May seek to use miraculous power for selfish ends.
3. Pride may become a problem and they stop giving the glory to God.
4. May attempt to produce miracles in their own strength.

TONGUES/INTERPRETATION OF TONGUES

Definition: **Tongues - A Holy Spirit-inspired utterance that enables a Christian to speak in a language unknown to the speaker, for the purpose of building up the worshipping body through its interpretation.**

Definition: **Interpretation of Tongues - The supernatural ability to interpret words spoken in tongues into the language of the listeners, so that the worshipping body can be built up.**

Gift Characteristics of Tongues:

1. Can be either known languages or angelic tongues (Acts 2:4 ff.; 1 Corinthians 13:1).
2. The only gift which cannot build up the Body of Christ by itself. It must have an interpretation to edify. It should not be used if the gift of interpretation is not shared in tandem.
3. May be a sign for non-Christians.
4. Are to be communicated alongside prophecy in an orderly manner (1 Corinthians 14:40).
5. Some speak in tongues with the laying on of hands.

Gift Characteristics for the Interpretation of Tongues:

1. God speaks to His people through the interpretation of a tongue.
2. Almost like a prophetic utterance or word of knowledge offered second-hand.
3. Will build the body.
4. Without this gift present, tongues should not be shared publicly.

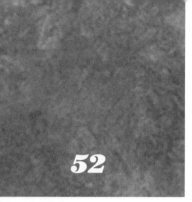

Gift Liabilities (together):

1. Because of the apparent ecstatic and emotional nature of the gift of tongues, expressions can get out of hand to dramatic proportions, as the Corinthians demonstrated.
2. People sometimes fake one or both of these gifts when pressured to exercise them.
3. The guidelines in 1 Corinthians 14 should be closely followed so that the Body of Christ can indeed be edified by this combination of gifts.
4. Paul would rather speak in five intelligible words than 10,000 in tongues. Tongues are not the ultimate gift.

WORD OF KNOWLEDGE

Definition: **The supernatural ability to receive and share revealed knowledge which was not otherwise known, or the ability to gather and clarify large quantities of Biblical knowledge with unusual spiritual insight.**

Gift Characteristics:

1. Has a clear sense of receiving messages from God.
2. May manifest itself by a sense of supernatural insight coming directly out of prayer.
3. Words, phrases or word pictures may commonly appear in their mind.
4. Understands or knows things that they did not know naturally.
5. Some would see this gift as the ability to research and combine large amounts of Biblical knowledge in a short period of time, with phenomenal understanding.

Gift Liabilities:

1. May respond to false or self-initiated impulses.
2. May inappropriately communicate a personal message for someone in a public setting (i.e. should have been shared personally because of the message's content).
3. Pride may grow because of the "great Biblical insights" discerned or messages received.
4. May mistakenly give a personal message to a large group of people, thus creating confusion for many people.

DEFINITIONS OF "OTHER POTENTIAL GIFTS"

Since many of the following "potential gifts" are included in the gifts survey, please take note that they may or may not be a spiritual gift. If two or three of your top six gifts are from this list, then add the next two or three highest gifts from your scoresheet.

Personal Notes

Celibacy: The supernatural capacity to remain contentedly single for the sake of the Gospel.

Creative Ability (craftsmanship or music): Because of key Old Testament references to these special skills in the building of the temple and the development of worship, some consider these as New Testament spiritual gifts.

Exorcism: The role of a Christian to cast out demons and evil spirits in the name of Jesus Christ.

Hospitality: The supernatural ability to open one's home freely and without reservation, even to strangers, for the purpose of serving those who are made welcome.

Intercession: The supernatural ability to pray for extended periods of time and see frequent and specific answers to prayers, much more so than the average Christian (taken from C. Peter Wagner, Your Spiritual Gifts Can Help Your Church Grow, Regal Books, Ventura, CA).

Martyrdom: The supernatural capacity to be willing to joyfully suffer and die for the sake of the Kingdom of God.

Missionary: A calling from God to exercise other spiritual gifts in a cross-cultural context.

Voluntary Poverty: The supernatural capacity to live in low economic status in order to identify with and minister to the poor and oppressed more effectively.

For the further input on these potential gifts, those which may be gifts but are not clearly mentioned in the New Testament, please use the appendix in one of Paul Ford's study guides on spiritual gifts: <u>Getting Your Gifts in Gear</u>

Dr. Paul R. Ford is a consultant, author, trainer and conference speaker committed to equipping and releasing the body of Christ to BE the Body of Christ. Paul is committed to his wife, Julie, and son, Stephen, at home in Albuquerque, New Mexico.

His ministry takes him from Los Angeles to Moscow and focuses on lay mobilization, leadership training, and team-building. His published works include the "Mobilizing Spiritual Gifts" series and the book Unleash Your Church! In his speaking and consulting ministry over the past five years, Paul has worked with more than 50 denominational and mission groups, 300 individual churches, and 6000+ Christian leaders.

Paul has a B.A. in Journalism from Tarkio College, Missouri, and an M. Div. from Fuller Theological Seminary, Pasadena, CA. He received his Doctor of Ministry Degree studying under C. Peter Wagner at Fuller. He is also an ordained pastor with 10+ years experience in local church ministry. All that he shares in his seminars and writings come from ministry experience in the field.